CENTRAL

Robert Goddard and the Liquid Rocket Engine

John Bankston

Mitchell Lane
PUBLISHERS

PO Box 619
Bear, Delaware 19701

Unlocking the Secrets of Science

Profiling 20th Century Achievers in Science, Medicine, and Technology

Robert Goddard and the Liquid Rocket Engine

Second Printing

Library of Congress Cataloging-in-Publication Data
Bankston, John, 1974-
    Robert Goddard and the liquid rocket engine/John Bankston.
        p. cm. — (Unlocking the secrets of science)
    Includes bibliographical references and index.
    ISBN 1-58415-107-2
    1. Goddard, Robert Hutchings, 1882-1945. 2. Rocketry—United States—
Biography. 3. Astronautics—United States—Biography. I. Title. II. Series.
TL781.85.G6 B36 2001
621.43'56'092—dc21
[B]   2001038372

ABOUT THE AUTHOR: Like Robert Goddard, John Bankston is a native of Massachusetts; he began publishing articles in newspapers and magazines while still a teenager. Since then, he has written over two hundred articles, and contributed chapters to books such as *Crimes of Passion* and *Death Row 2000*, which have been sold in bookstores around the world. He has recently written a number of biographies for Mitchell Lane including books on Mandy Moore, Jessica Simpson and Jonas Salk. He currently lives in Los Angeles, California, pursuing a career in the entertainment industry. He has worked as a writer for the movies *Dot-Com* and the upcoming *Planetary Suicide*, which begins filming in 2002. As an actor John has appeared in episodes of *Sabrina the Teenage Witch*, *Charmed* and *Get Real* along with appearances in the films *Boys and Girls*, and *America So Beautiful*. He has a supporting part in *Planetary Suicide* and has recently completed his first young adult novel, *18 To Look Younger*.

PHOTO CREDITS: cover: p. 6 Archive Photos; p. 10 Science Photo Library; p. 16 Globe Photos; p. 22 NASA/Mark Marten; p. 28 Barbara Marvis; p.34 Archive Photos; p. 38 Archive Photos; p. 44 Archive Photos; p. 49 Barbara Marvis.

PUBLISHER'S NOTE: In selecting those persons to be profiled in this series, we first attempted to identify the most notable accomplishments of the 20th century in science, medicine, and technology. When we were done, we noted a serious deficiency in the inclusion of women. For the greater part of the 20th century science, medicine, and technology were male-dominated fields. In many cases, the contributions of women went unrecognized. Women have tried for years to be included in these areas, and in many cases, women worked side by side with men who took credit for their ideas and discoveries. Even as we move forward into the 21st century, we find women still sadly underrepresented. It is not an oversight, therefore, that we profiled mostly male achievers. Information simply does not exist to include a fair selection of women.

Contents

Robert Goddard stands beside "Nell" his prototype liquid fueled rocket prior to its first successful test flight on March 16, 1926, in Auburn, Massachusetts.

Chapter 1

Space...The Final Frontier

● ●

Most people think that the first people landed on the moon in the summer of 1969. American astronaut Neil Armstrong climbed backward down a short ladder from the lunar module he had piloted and set foot on the moon's surface on July 20 at exactly 10:56 p.m. Eastern Daylight Time. Millions of people heard him make his famous statement, "That's one small step for a man, one giant leap for mankind."

But exactly a century earlier, in 1869, other men stood on the moon. They too made the long flight from the earth that Armstrong would take 100 years later.

The difference is that Armstrong actually made the flight to the moon. The earlier "landing" existed only in the imagination of a famous French author named Jules Verne. His two novels which describe manned flights to the moon, *Around the Moon* (published in 1869) and the earlier *From the Earth to the Moon* (1865), were very popular.

Imagination means picturing the impossible and dreaming of possibilities. Imagination is what drives discovery. It was probably more important in the development of space travel than in any other field of science.

In ancient times, people created mythological stories to describe the bright lights dancing and twinkling in the night sky. They saw stars as the backbone of a beast, the moon as a white bird, the sky as a curved roof. They pictured gods and goddesses, warriors and animals soaring through the heavens.

Yet even thousands of years ago, some people looked upwards and began to see those lights in terms closer to science than mythology. For example, the Ionians were Greeks who lived on the shores of Asia Minor (modern-day Turkey) in 600 BC. They used the stars to guide them in their voyages across the Mediterranean Sea. So even though the first space travelers didn't arrive for another 2,600 years, it is fitting that the name we use to describe them comes from two Greek words: "astro" for stars and "nauts" for sailors. Astronauts are literally "star sailors."

For many centuries, people were exploring the earth, constantly pushing the boundaries of the known world further and further. The "New World" wasn't discovered until 1492. Until the end of the 19th century, much of Africa was known as "Darkest Africa." And no one set foot on the North and South Poles until 1909 and 1912.

With almost every square inch of the earth finally mapped and explored, humans wanted new "worlds" to explore. Not surprisingly, they began looking upward. By looking up on a clear night sky and imagining navigating stars and planets, some people dreamed of space vehicles— everything from hot-air balloons to rockets shot from a cannon.

Despite these dreams, however, many respected scientists believed that space travel was impossible.

But Verne's books were still popular, and they helped to inspire three visionaries separated by thousands of miles.

Russian mathematician Konstantin Tsiolkovsky was a deaf teacher living in an isolated town when he used complicated formulas to prove travel outside the earth's atmosphere was possible. He struggled with many different shapes and designs before deciding a rocket would be the best way to escape our planet's gravity.

In Germany, Hermann Oberth wrote a book describing manned space flight and helped a famous German director named Fritz Lang put this vision on movie screens.

The third visionary didn't just write about rockets. He built them.

A sickly boy, he spent a childhood suffering from pneumonia, bronchitis, and numerous other ailments. Illness held him back for two years in high school, and isolated him from his peers. Not surprisingly, books became his closest companions. When he was a child, he read Verne's novels. As a teen he would be inspired by another writer, H.G. Wells, whose stories about a Martian attack were published in the *Boston Post*. He believed that someday men would be able to fly into outer space in rockets.

So when he grew up, he tested his rockets on rural farms in Massachusetts and the desert expanses of New Mexico despite doubt and ridicule from others. He refused to listen to the teachers, the scientists, the experts who told him the dreams of Wells and Verne were fantasies created to sell books.

Robert Goddard worked in almost complete isolation as he developed a liquid fueled rocket, which would light a path along the sky and blaze a trail of discovery. Goddard's inventions would lead to that summer day in 1969 when Neil Armstrong set his foot upon another world. Robert Goddard proved the dreams of Verne and Wells were possible.

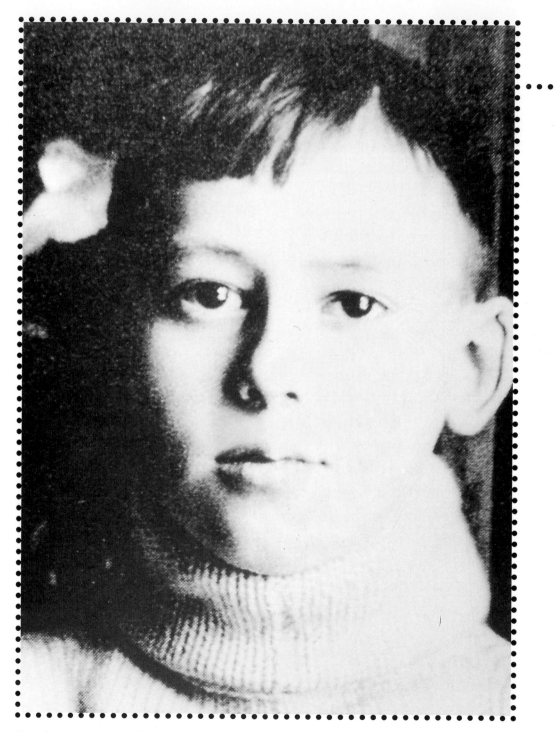

By eleven years old, Robert Goddard had already endured numerous illnesses and developed a fascination with space travel.

Chapter 2

A Rocket From a Cherry Tree

• •

Five-year-old Robert Goddard was ready to fly. He'd taken a zinc rod from a Leclanche battery and held onto it as he scuffed his feet along the gravel sidewalk in front of his house. He'd seen how shuffling his feet on the carpet created sparks and static electricity. He'd paid attention to how the battery worked. Now he hoped he could generate enough energy to send him flying.

Maybe he'd make it all the way into outer space.

His mother, Fanny, stepped in just in time. Though she managed to prevent one dangerous experiment, there would be many others. By the time he was a teenager, almost nothing would stop him.

Scientific curiosity ran in the family.

Robert's father Nahum subscribed to *Scientific American*, a magazine that described the latest discoveries and research. Nahum was fascinated by the changes taking place in the late 1800s, from light bulbs to movie cameras.

Nahum worked as an accountant when his only child—Robert Hutchings Goddard—was born on October 5, 1882 in Worcester, Massachusetts. The state's second largest city, Worcester is about forty miles from Boston.

A few months after Robert was born, Nahum decided to take a risk. He abandoned the security of his accounting job and moved the family to Roxbury, a Boston suburb. He and Simeon Stubbs formed a company called Stubbs and Goddard, which manufactured specialty knives. Nahum Goddard's work involved traveling around the region selling the product.

Although he was very busy and often away from home, he always made time for Robert. When Robert was younger, Nahum would read to him from *Scientific American*. As his son got older, the pair would buy the latest telephones and phonograph players described by the magazine.

The Goddards were "early adopters." Early adopters are the first people to use new technology and buy new products. They are "the first on the block" to purchase the latest innovations, even if the latest is more expensive or less reliable. The thrill of trying out new technology makes up for any disappointments.

In the 1980s, early adopters were the first to use cellular phones, fax machines and VCRs.

In the 1880s, the Goddards were the first on their block to use electric lights and a gas-powered car.

When Robert was fifteen, his mother contracted tuberculosis, a serious lung disease. In the 1890s, many people who got the disease died from it, and there was no cure. Doctors advised patients to avoid moist environments like coastal Boston. Goddard sold his half of the business to his partner and moved the family inland, back to Worcester.

Fanny wasn't the only one sick.

Robert was always fighting one illness or another. He mainly suffered from bronchitis and pneumonia, diseases that affect the lungs. Robert would get better, go back to school and then a few months later become sick again. He was always weaker than the other kids and because of his illness he didn't spend much time with children his own age. Since he didn't have any brothers or sisters, most of his company came from adults. Because of this, he was usually more at ease around older people.

Robert's escape lay in his own imagination, and in the books he read. When he was younger, Robert was inspired by Jules Verne's stories about space travel. While he lay in bed, Robert would spend hours reading *From the Earth to the Moon* and *Round the Moon.* He'd imagine that he was no longer confined to the house in Maple Hill, that he was able to explore worlds millions of miles from earth.

Robert Goddard didn't just enjoy the author's flights of fancy. He studied Verne's descriptions, scribbling notes in the books' margins on whether or not the writer's ideas seemed possible. This questioning attitude—skepticism— was excellent training for the budding scientist.

Although he found the works of the 19th century novelist interesting, it took a more current writer—England's H.G. Wells—to truly inspire young Goddard.

In his mid-teens, Goddard waited eagerly for "Fighters from Mars, or The War of the Worlds, In and Near Boston," a serial which was published daily in his hometown paper, *The Boston Post.* Wells' descriptions played a major role in Goddard's decision to devote himself to space flight.

"The spell of *The War of the Worlds* was complete about a year afterward," the scientist mentioned in a letter to Wells years later, "and I decided that what might conservatively be called 'high altitude research' was the most fascinating problem in existence."

Wells would write back to Goddard, in a letter the scientist proudly showed friends and visitors.

Goddard didn't just read. He *tried.* From those early steps with batteries to nearly blowing up the house eleven years later when an attempt to turn graphite into diamonds using a combination of hydrogen and oxygen failed, Goddard never stopped experimenting.

Many of his ideas were about leaving the earth. He dreamed of escaping gravity, that mysterious force discovered by Sir Isaac Newton which binds all of us to this planet. Newton, a curious Englishman whose work has driven many modern scientific discoveries, wrote about the laws of gravity after an apple hit him on the head in 1666.

Goddard's desire to fly away from the planet led him to build a crude balloon and convince a druggist to fill it with hydrogen gas. Like the batteries and the attempt to make diamonds, the balloon didn't work. But Goddard didn't let his lack of success stop him. "Failior [failure] crowns enterprise," he wrote in an early notebook, showing as much imagination in his spelling as he did in his experiments. Robert believed that each failure was a necessary step on the journey to success; every time he failed it meant he was that much closer to succeeding. First, however, he had to graduate from high school.

Despite his interest in science, math was one of Goddard's worst subjects. He struggled and struggled to understand. He knew he needed a strong background in mathematics in order to get into a good college and focus on science. Unfortunately, no matter how hard he struggled, his grades were poor. The many days, even months, of school absences due to illness didn't help.

In the end, it took competition from a smart classmate to drive Robert to succeed. The fact that she was a girl, at a time when girls weren't expected to even be interested in math, finally drove him to study. Eventually, he not only learned his subject but also wrote a small book on geometry. He earned the highest grade in his class—not because he was the brightest, but because he worked the hardest.

On October 19, 1899, Goddard was feeling healthy enough to prune some branches on a cherry tree in his grandmother's orchard. His mind wandered. "It was one of the quiet, colorful afternoons of sheer beauty which we have in October in New England," Goddard would later recall in an interview, "and as I looked towards the fields at the east, I imagined how wonderful it would be to make some device which had even the possibility of ascending to Mars, and how it would look on a small scale, if sent up from the meadow at my feet."

In the sky he imagined a device like something from Wells' story. This machine would have two horizontal shafts which spun at each end, with two great weights at the tips. The one above spun much faster than the one below.

"I was a different boy when I descended the tree than from when I ascended," Goddard would later write of the experience.

Robert Goddard would always remember the date of October 19, calling it his "Anniversary Day" and celebrating it the same way a happily married man celebrates his wedding anniversary. It was the day he realized he wanted to some day build his own spaceship!

Although stories like The War of the Worlds *were considered nothing more than science fiction by many, the writings of novelist H.G. Wells inspired Robert Goddard to devote his life to what he called "high altitude research."*

Chapter 3

The Rocket Man

At age twenty-one, Robert Goddard was one of the oldest seniors at South High School. It was illness, not poor grades, which had slowed him down, but Robert planned to make up for lost time.

In 1904, he graduated at the top of his class. Goddard was ready to pursue science as a career. He was also ready to abandon the dreams he now considered childish.

"By the time I graduated from High School," Goddard recalled, "I had a set of models which would not work and a number of suggestions which, from the physics I had learned, I now knew were erroneous [wrong]. Accordingly, one day I gathered together all the notes I could find and burned them in the little wood stove in the dining room."

Robert Goddard was ready for a fresh start.

At first, the Goddard family wasn't sure they would even be able to send their son to college. Fanny's battle with tuberculosis had been very expensive and money was tight after Nahum sold his portion of the knife business. In the end, Robert's grandmother, Mary, who owned the cherry orchard where he'd found inspiration as a teen, borrowed the money for his higher education.

Provided with the loan from his grandmother, Robert enrolled in nearby Worcester Polytechnic Institute. The school trained civil engineers; its graduates built bridges, roads and buildings. It wasn't a typical school for a future scientist, but Robert was trying to be practical. He was trying to forget about rockets. He studied hard and kept his more unconventional ideas to himself.

Despite the school's seriousness, there were opportunities for Robert to be creative. As a freshman, he wrote an essay called "Traveling in 1950," which imagined a vacuum tube railroad in which the passenger cars would be propelled by magnetic power. In the distant future of 1950, Goddard described a ten-minute commute from Boston to New York City.

Although Goddard was used to spending most of his time alone, he did well making friends. He was popular enough to be elected class president and was editor of the school paper, *Aftermath*. He even wrote both lyrics and music for a new school song, "Old Tech."

Goddard proved himself outside of school as well. He developed an essay from English class about gyroscopes—spinning wheels that helped in navigation—and submitted it to his father's favorite magazine, *Scientific American*. Goddard was barely a college sophomore when the article appeared.

Encouraged, Goddard decided to revisit some of the ideas he'd had in high school. He devoted hours away from school work to writing another essay he called "On the Possibility of Navigating Interplanetary Space." *Scientific American* wasn't interested. Neither were *Popular Science Monthly* nor *Popular Astronomy*. All three of the magazines had the same response: they dealt with fact, not fiction. Goddard's ideas belonged in a novel.

In 1947, Edward G. Pendray wrote in his book *The Coming Age of Rocket Power* that "During the period when for the first time it was really undergoing something like genuine scientific development, the rocket was to become, to many unthinking people, a symbol of impractical ideas and fantastic schemes."

Still, no matter how hard Goddard tried to concentrate on other subjects and other interests, thoughts of rockets filled his mind. "God pity a one dream man!" he jotted angrily in his diary.

According to one account, Goddard was watching a Fourth of July fireworks display when he realized rockets would be the best way for him to achieve his dreams of space flight. Balloons were bound by our atmosphere, that invisible boundary of air circling the earth. Maybe a rocket could propel a traveler beyond the reaches of the planet's gravity and atmosphere.

Rockets were not new. They had been invented by the Chinese around the year 1,000 AD, soon after the development of gunpowder. Rockets were packed full of this explosive substance and then set off. They were used in both fireworks displays and combat. One legend describes China's Wan-Hu, who tied himself to forty-seven firecrackers which he set off in an attempt to reach the moon. Even in the legend, it didn't work.

By Goddard's time, versions of a rocket designed by a British military officer named William Congreve in 1791 were still in use. "The rocket's red glare" in our national anthem refers to an attack on Fort McHenry in Baltimore harbor during the War of 1812 using Congreve rockets.

But they weren't very accurate and by Goddard's time their main use was on ships as distress signals and to carry lines to shore. Only novelists, and a few scientists like Goddard, imagined that rockets could be used for space travel.

He returned to writing his ideas in notebooks. In 1906, he imagined a rocket powered by the sun. In 1907, he considered launching a rocket from a high flying balloon.

That same year, he secretly descended to the musty basement laboratory in his school's physics building. He brought with him a small powder-fueled rocket which he intended to test. When he accidentally set it off, the entire building quickly filled with thick, acrid smoke.

Goddard was lucky. Instead of expelling him, school officials encouraged the budding scientist to continue his experiments. "Just be a little more careful," they told him.

In his senior year, Goddard's fellow students voted him "The Brightest" in their class. Worcester Polytechnic seemed to agree, hiring Goddard as a part-time teacher in 1908, the same year he earned his Bachelor of Science degree. Many of his students described Goddard as inspirational. Unlike many professors, he was interested in his students' opinions even if they contradicted the popular beliefs of the time.

Even while teaching, Goddard continued to work on his ideas for rocket flight.

It became an obsession, taking up all of his free time. The year after his graduation from Worcester Polytechnic, he settled on using a modified artillery rocket. However, these rockets were powered by gunpowder, which is a solid fuel. Goddard realized liquid fuel could burn hotter and allow the rocket to reach the high speeds necessary to escape the earth's atmosphere. Liquid fuel could be also turned on or off, because its flow didn't need to be constant.

Goddard remembered his failed graphite experiments as a teenager involving hydrogen and oxygen gas. As a liquid, hydrogen was highly explosive and could lift the rocket from the earth's atmosphere. Since oxygen is needed to keep fuel burning, liquid oxygen would be used because there wasn't any oxygen outside of earth's atmosphere.

He made calculations based on those chemical elements in their liquid state. Relying on both estimates and mathematical formulas, Goddard roughly calculated that he would need about 45 pounds of fuel to lift one pound into space. On New Year's Eve he listed 26 rocket-related items. It was Goddard's scientific New Year's resolution.

He decided he didn't care what others thought about his interests. He would do everything he could to develop a rocket. And there would be no more burning of notebooks. Eventually, his writings would fill nearly thirty very thick volumes.

The problem was that the fuels were expensive and unstable. There was a good chance the entire rocket would burn up. The very means of powering the rocket could also destroy it.

Goddard's burning scientific curiosity held the same sort of power. For while his overwhelming need to discover and experiment was a kind of fuel, it would soon come close to destroying the young scientist.

Not just a scientist, but a teacher as well, Robert Goddard taught at Clark University in Massachusetts for much of his adult life and was considered by many students to be an inspiring, open-minded professor.

Chapter 4

Two Weeks to Live!

• •

Robert Goddard made up for all the time he lost in high school by earning his Ph.D. degree from nearby Clark University in just three years. His doctorate in physics— the study of matter, energy and the way the two interact— would take most students twice as long to complete. In many ways Goddard had a gifted education. His doctorate in physics gave him an understanding of how objects like rockets would behave. His engineering degree gave him the know-how to build them.

Few scientists possessed this type of educational combination.

After his graduation from Clark, Goddard was an "honorary fellow," an unpaid position which allowed him to use the university's labs for his research. During this time, Goddard invented a vacuum tube oscillator, a device for measuring the electric current which traveled through the tube.

This important development in the world of electrical engineering led to an invitation from Harvard University. The oldest university in the United States, Harvard was part of the Ivy League, a group of eastern colleges considered tops in both academic and social prestige. As a graduate of smaller, less well-known Clark, Goddard was nervous when officials from Harvard asked him to give a speech about his research.

Despite his nerves, Goddard knew what an honor it was and agreed to go. So in 1912, Goddard traveled to the nearby Cambridge campus and spoke before an audience of mainly older scientists. Among them was Dr. W.F. Magie, the dean of New Jersey's Princeton University, another Ivy League school. He was so impressed with Goddard's knowledge of his subject that after the speech he offered the young man a job as a research instructor.

Goddard quickly accepted. After years of study and hard work, he finally had a well-paying job, one with access to a world-class lab. He also planned to continue his own private rocket research.

He began at Princeton in the fall of 1912, initially working on experiments similar to those he'd described in his paper "Traveling in 1950." His work with magnetic fields occupied only his days, as his nights were filled with increasingly complicated calculations on every imaginable aspect of rocket travel. Most accounts describe Robert as getting less than four hours of sleep each night.

For a young man who'd been a sickly adolescent, it was a prescription for trouble. As 1912 turned into 1913, Goddard began having bouts of weakness, dizziness and coughing. He continued to push himself, believing he was too close to a solution to quit. In his mind he could already see his rocket lifting off from the ground. He filled page after page as he tried to determine how to accomplish his dreams.

Though Goddard got sicker, he refused to stop. During his spring break, he traveled home to see his family. His fever spiked and his cough got worse. Concerned, his parents convinced Goddard that he needed to be looked at by a doctor.

A group of doctors arrived at the Goddard family house and examined him. The symptoms were obvious. Goddard had tuberculosis, the same disease that had sickened his mother.

Because he had put off seeking treatment for so long, the condition had become even worse. After the examination, the doctors spoke quietly to each other before reaching the same conclusion.

Robert Goddard would probably be dead within two weeks.

Goddard and his parents listened as the doctors offered some hope. If Robert Goddard slept on the family porch to breathe the cold air of spring, if he rested, if he didn't do any work, then maybe—but just maybe—he might live.

When the doctors left, Goddard made his decision. Perhaps he figured he had nothing else to lose. Perhaps his scientific skepticism colored his belief in the doctors. Regardless of the reason, Goddard basically did the exact opposite of everything the doctors asked.

Instead of sleeping on the porch, he stayed inside where he would be warm. Instead of rest, he rose before dawn each morning and hiked along his family's property. Instead of avoiding work, he began to read in earnest, hiding his books beneath his mattress whenever the doctors visited.

And instead of dying, Goddard got better. The young man's recovery in the face of so many negative opinions strengthened Goddard's belief in himself.

Instead of going back to Princeton, Goddard took a part-time job at Clark as a physics professor. The thirty-year-old moved back home, returning to his childhood room. In many ways he also returned to his childhood dreams.

Dr. Robert Goddard dreamed of rockets.

"In the fall of 1914," Goddard would later write in one of his many notebooks, "while teaching part time at Clark, I worked out the theory and calculations for smokeless powder and hydrogen and oxygen completely and began experiments on the efficiency of ordinary rockets. Curiously enough, the initial mass needed to send 1 lb. to infinity for hydrogen and oxygen at 50 per cent efficiency, namely 43.5 lbs., was close to that estimated roughly at 45 lbs. on January 31, 1909."

Ideas he'd scarcely examined just five years before were actually very close to what Goddard was now able to prove. In 1914, using the information he'd developed over the last decade, Goddard applied for two patents. The patents would prove that he was the first to develop what would later be known as Goddard's liquid fueled rocket.

The two patent applications included drawings which covered three new ideas. The first described a rocket combustion chamber. In some ways the principle is similar to an automobile engine. In a car, gasoline inside the engine creates a controlled explosion, called combustion, which provides energy and makes the car run.

In a similar way, the rocket combustion chamber Goddard designed would allow the fuels to burn. A nozzle would then let the exhaust gases created by the burning fuel escape. This action would provide thrust—the upward flight of a rocket.

Goddard's second development was to feed fuel into the rocket's combustion chamber as a way of creating either steady or interrupted force, depending on the need.

The third innovation was a multiple-stage rocket. This was the way Goddard solved the problem of carrying so much fuel in order to have liftoff—when a rocket escapes the atmosphere. When the fuel in the first stage was consumed, that section would separate from the rest of the rocket.

This principle has been used successfully throughout the space program, including the current launches of the space shuttle.

In 1914, Goddard was awarded the two patents, the first of over two hundred he'd receive in his lifetime. For the next seventeen years, no one else could copy, manufacture, or sell the rockets he designed without his permission.

The patents were just a first step. For over a decade, he had spent his free time making notes, using a series of complex calculations to describe the workings of rockets he could only imagine.

Now Dr. Robert Goddard wanted to do more than just describe rockets. He wanted to build them.

Standing before an image of the moon is a wax figure of Robert Goddard and his rocket that led the way to Neil Armstrong's first steps on Earth's distant satellite. This display is shown at the Goddard Space Flight Visitor Center in Greenbelt, Maryland.

Chapter 5

The Rocket's Red Glare

• •

Still weak from his bout with tuberculosis, Goddard returned to a part-time position at Clark University and a full-time dream of rocket flight. Even before the patents were issued, he'd begun receiving dozens of packages containing all kinds of rockets: Chinese rockets, British Congreve rockets, fireworks, and flares. He also purchased a number of the most readily available rocket, which was used for signaling by ships in trouble.

Unfortunately, this rocket was very inefficient and slow. So instead of testing it outdoors, Goddard brought the rocket into his lab, and held it down with a steel chamber connected to a test stand. He tried different types of nozzles, and fed them a smokeless powder. In this way he could test a rocket indoors. Still, many of his fellow professors worried that solitary Goddard might some day blow up the school.

Goddard was careful. He didn't want a repeat of that smoky experiment in his college physics building.

During this time, Goddard also solved one of the most important puzzles relating to rocket flight. Scientists in the early twentieth century debated whether or not a rocket could actually fly into outer space. They believed that as rockets hurtled through the airless expanse they would have nothing to push against.

Here Dr. Goddard referred to Newton's third law of motion: for every action, there is an equal and opposite reaction. The action of the rocket firing should have a reaction—hopefully the rocket moving forward.

Goddard decided to test his theory with a pistol. He set up an airless chamber called a vacuum tube and placed the gun inside. When he fired, the bullet wouldn't have an "atmosphere" to push against. Goddard conducted his test. Not only did the pistol fire, but the bullet also traveled faster compared to normal conditions! He believed a rocket would behave the same way.

As he later told a reporter with the *Boston Sunday Advertiser*, "The phenomenon is easily understood if one thinks of ejected gas as a charge of fine shot moving with a very high velocity. The chamber will react or 'kick' when the charge is fired, exactly as a shotgun 'kicks' when firing a charge of ordinary shot."

With his patents in place and his lab tests going well, Goddard realized he was ready to begin construction of his own rocket. Throughout 1915, Goddard had begun firing his own versions—rockets which used the designs he'd patented.

Robert Goddard would wake up early, before dawn, and hike out to nearby Coes Pond. Before first light, he'd fire his prototypes, or test models, out over the still water, watching as they arced across the sky, their fiery red tails mimicking the sunrise.

Unfortunately the greatest challenge the scientist faced was no longer a lack of belief among his peers, although that still existed. It was lack of money.

Goddard was paying for the rockets out of his own pocket, because the university wasn't funding his research.

In 1916, Goddard decided to appeal to the Smithsonian Institution in Washington, DC. Founded by Englishman James Smithson in 1846, this organization dedicated to "the increase and diffusion of knowledge among men" had earlier funded the work of Samuel P. Langley. Langley, then the head of the Smithsonian, had used the money to conduct a number of important experiments with the first airplanes.

Goddard wrote a very careful letter, discussing only the advantages of rockets for research in the upper atmosphere, where balloons couldn't go. He described how successful his previous experiments had been, calling them "truly remarkable." Most important, he avoided any of the more fantastical terms which had earlier led to rejection by various magazines.

The response was swift. Dr. Charles D. Walcott, the Smithsonian's secretary, wrote back and asked Goddard to provide more detail. Goddard didn't take any chances. He aimed to impress. So the scientist presented Walcott with a leather-bound volume, which covered his theories on rocket flight and the experiments he hoped to conduct. The embossed gold title read "A Method of Reaching Extreme Altitudes."

It was perfect timing. The Smithsonian had just received a donation from Thomas G. Hodgkins. It specifically required that half the money be used on "atmospheric research," which was the exact topic of Goddard's proposal.

Four months later, Goddard got his grant of one thousand dollars immediately and another four thousand "as needed." That was an extraordinary amount of money in 1916 and Goddard didn't waste any time putting it to good use.

"I'm just a little dog with a great big bone," Goddard would often remark modestly to other scientists. Still, he had a great deal of belief in his experiment's potential.

"He knew precisely what he was doing," Walcott said in a later interview. "I have never seen so much confidence."

That confidence would be sorely tested by the events of 1917.

World War I was already devastating Europe when the United States joined the Allied forces. In June, General

"Black Jack" Pershing led the first wave of American soldiers overseas, where they joined up with troops from France, England, and Canada.

The Smithsonian recommended Goddard to the Navy Signal Corps, thinking the scientist's innovations might help the war effort. In the beginning of 1918, Goddard traveled to Washington, DC and met with government officials. He proposed a recoilless rocket launcher, a weapon which would be hand-held and not have a "kick." Twenty-five years later, Goddard's ideas would lead to the bazooka, a similarly hand-held rocket launcher which would prove to be an effective weapon against tanks.

The military shared the Smithsonian's belief in the young scientist. He was given $20,000 to develop his ideas. Goddard returned to his old college, the Worcester Polytechnic Institute. He worked with two graduate students, H.S. Parker and Clarence Hickman. It was Hickman who would go on to be the main developer of the bazooka.

The three men worked tirelessly. Goddard realized that he was no longer striving towards a distant fantasy of space travel. Now he needed to succeed quickly, because he knew thousands of American lives might be saved if he developed this weapon.

In June, Goddard and his two assistants were posted to Pasadena, California. The three men spent a long, hot summer at the Mount Wilson Solar Observatory. In just a few months, Goddard was ready to give a demonstration.

In an interview, Dr. Charles C. Abbott, Walcott's successor at the Smithsonian, recalled the day.

"Dr. Goddard brought with him a projectile which looked like a regular three-inch artillery shell, brass cartridge and all. It was comparatively light in weight. There was no gun, no carriage; simply this strange looking shell—a rocket.

"Carefully, Dr. Goddard laid this shell on a wooden table, which was resting on the ground. There was no bracing, no base against which the shell could recoil. A slender wire was attached. Before the table... sandbags used in the best trench defenses, capable of stopping machine gun and Army rifle bullets....

"'Are you ready, gentlemen?' asked Goddard. They were. There was a low crackle of electricity, a loud swish. The brass shell of the rocket trembled, spurted fire, and the projectile hurled outward, into the sandbags."

Still impressed years later, Abbott would remember, "An examination revealed the rocket had penetrated three sandbags, and the light brass shell didn't even fall off the table."

Just a few days later, on November 11, 1918, Germany surrendered. The sudden peace would be celebrated by everyone, although for Goddard the end of the war meant the end of government funding for his rockets. He boarded a train and made the long trip back to Massachusetts. He realized that even with all the money the government had given him, building a working liquid fueled rocket was quite different from describing one in mathematical formulas and patent application drawings.

Dr. Goddard realized that the path to developing his ideas would be a long, slow one. Like the tortoise that wins the race, Goddard knew slow and steady was the only way to go.

He also knew that in order to succeed, he would have to keep his ideas about space flight quiet.

Unfortunately, Goddard's hope for quiet, anonymous research would soon be destroyed.

Alone with his rocket—Robert Goddard preferred to work without supervision and was reluctant to share his ideas. Sometimes this kept him from being accepted by the scientific community.

Chapter 6

Fly Me to the Moon

• •

Because Goddard was an only child, he was used to being alone. He didn't like having supervisors looking over his shoulder, picking apart his work. He labored by himself at his lab table. He wrote down the results of his experiments in notebooks only he saw.

Dr. Arthur G. Webster had overseen Goddard's doctoral work. He knew the scientist's nature. When Webster took over the position of director of Clark University's physics department, he was filling a job held by A.A. Michelson, who had been the first American scientist to win a Nobel Prize. Webster wanted to lead Clark's physics department to similar fame. He saw Goddard as the school's best hope.

Webster bluntly told Goddard that if he didn't publish his work with the Smithsonian, then Webster would do it himself and claim that it was his own work.

Goddard looked over the paper he'd written. Reluctantly, he decided to see if the research institution would publish it. They quickly agreed.

In January of 1920, Goddard received the skinny volume, cheaply bound in brown paper and entitled "A Method of Reaching Extreme Altitudes." Most of the other 1,750 copies would be stored at the Smithsonian. Goddard figured he'd seen the last of the book. He was wrong.

On January 12, Goddard awoke to find that his work had become a front page story. In his hometown paper, *The Boston American*, the headline screamed, "Modern Jules Verne Invents Rocket to Reach Moon." The Smithsonian had contacted newspapers across the country. Most of them ignored everything in the book, except for the last section where Goddard described how a rocket could someday travel to the moon. People quickly began volunteering to take the first flight to the moon, as if the rocket was sitting in Goddard's back yard, waiting to be fueled up and launched.

But in the early 1920s, the idea was beyond crazy. The *New York Times* said in an editorial that Goddard "does not know the relation of action to reaction and the need to have something better than a vacuum, against which to react... of course he only seems to lack the knowledge ladled out daily in high schools."

The writer wasn't just being mean. He was wrong. Goddard had already used a pistol to prove a rocket could travel forward in a vacuum.

In Massachusetts, Goddard was slowly developing a liquid fueled rocket. The differences between this rocket and one powered by solid fuel were enormous. Early rockets could be launched by touching a match to a fuse. The most complex part was the exhaust nozzle at the rocket's bottom which allowed escaping gas to lift the rocket.

A liquid fueled rocket would need a cooling system so the object wouldn't blow up under the extreme heat it would generate. A gunpowder rocket was sometimes fairly fragile, but a liquid fueled rocket needed to be solidly built because the burning fuel would create tremendous pressure.

The challenge was that if the liquid oxygen grew warm it would vaporize—turn into a gas and disappear. Then it would be useless. So Goddard developed the innovation of running super-cold liquid oxygen through a metal jacket which surrounded the combustion chamber.

Around 1918, Goddard had begun allowing a bright honors student named Esther Kisk to compile his notes and answer his letters. In 1924, Goddard married her.

In many ways, the two had as much a scientific partnership as a marriage. Esther took on certain duties for the scientist, from answering letters to maintaining the parachutes which helped the rockets safely return to earth.

A little after a year following their marriage, Goddard finished a rocket. It was about ten and a half feet long and weighed ten pounds. He spent several months checking it for leaks and testing it. Goddard had decided upon gasoline, rather than hydrogen, in part because gas was cheaper and more readily available. The combustion chamber and nozzle were at the top of the rocket, connected by long pipes to tanks of gasoline and liquid oxygen.

Early on the morning of March 16, 1926, the Goddards, along with Henry Sachs from Clark's instrument lab and assistant professor of physics Dr. P.M. Roope, loaded a trailer with the prototype rocket, which he had nicknamed "Nell," and headed for a farm owned by "Aunt" Effie Ward, who was called aunt, even by those not related to her.

His wife knelt in the snow and took what became a famous picture of Goddard standing next to the rocket. Sachs used a blowtorch on the end of a long pole to ignite the engine. A hot, white smokeless flame burst from the rocket's nozzle. Goddard held the release cord in his hand, waiting for the rocket to build up power.

After a minute, Goddard pulled the cord. Nothing. A minute went by.

And then, the rocket shot up into the sky at sixty miles per hour, sailing 184 feet in two and a half seconds.

Dr. Robert Goddard had done it. Like the Wright Brothers at Kitty Hawk, whose dreams were given life in the limping flight of the first working airplane, Goddard's decades of imaginative theories became reality in a launch that ended in less time than it takes to draw a breath.

World famous for completing the first transatlantic solo flight, pilot Charles Lindbergh helped Robert Goddard get the funding he needed to build his rockets in the 1930s.

Chapter 7
Roswell

A lthough Dr. Goddard tried again a few days later, this time he didn't publicize the four-second flight. After his embarrassment with the Smithsonian publications, he kept his experiments quiet and they didn't attract any attention from the press. Despite his reluctance to publish his findings, the Smithsonian continued to fund Goddard's work.

In July of 1926, he got a grant of $6,500 so he could build a larger rocket. Because it was bigger, the device could carry more fuel, and Goddard hoped it would reach a greater altitude. The rocket he designed had a larger steel frame, an improved combustion chamber and tanks which held twenty times the fuel. Goddard also moved a sixty-foot windmill onto the Ward farm. He used the structure to hold down the rocket until it lifted off.

At first Goddard's efforts led to little more than a series of spectacular explosions. Gas tanks blew up, valves melted, the combustion chamber burned. Goddard kept trying. "Failior crowns enterprise" was still his motto.

On July 17, 1929, he tested a rocket which was twelve feet long and weighed thirty pounds without the fuel. He loaded it with a camera and a barometer, a device to measure air pressure. This was the first rocket to carry instruments.

The device managed to soar one hundred feet before the gas tank exploded in a burst of flames which colored the sky and an explosion which could be heard for miles. The blast attracted the attention of neighbors, fire fighters, police and Goddard's old enemies—newspaper reporters. The local paper ran a headline that said "Moon Rocket Misses Target by 238,799 1/2 Miles." Once again his experiments would be global news even as he was warned to stop testing on the Ward farm or face jail.

The threat didn't matter. One of the many readers of the newspaper accounts was pilot Charles Lindbergh.

Lindbergh had his own fascination with flight. In May of 1927, the accomplished pilot had flown by himself from the United States to Paris, the first solo transatlantic flight in history. It made him as famous as a movie star, as powerful as a politician.

When he read about Goddard's rocket tests, Lindbergh knew he had to get involved. "If we're ever going beyond airplanes, we'll probably have to go to rockets," Lindbergh would later tell a friend.

The pilot traveled to Goddard's home and listened to Goddard discuss his experiments with liquid fueled rockets and his problems with local authorities. Then Goddard told him how much he'd need for full-time rocket research.

Twenty-five thousand dollars!

Lindbergh believed it would be worth it. He got in touch with Harry Guggenheim, whose wealthy family had founded the Guggenheim Fund for the Promotion of Aeronautics with three million dollars. Harry Guggenheim agreed to fund Goddard for the next four years.

Goddard had to leave Massachusetts. The state was his home, but it was a terrible place to test a rocket. He needed a place with plenty of wide open spaces, with clear, sunny days and little fog or cloud cover. A meteorologist, or weatherman, helped him find the perfect location.

Roswell, which is now famous for its rumored alien landings and a popular TV show, is located on the southeast corner of New Mexico. In 1930, Goddard and his wife left on a long, hot summer drive. A freight car carrying several assistants and the rocket parts would meet them at their new home.

By then the move wasn't just for science. It was for his health. Goddard's lungs had always been weak and as he got older, the condition got worse. He hoped the dry heat of New Mexico would do him some good.

Esther and Robert Goddard settled into a stone house on Mescalero Ranch. Goddard convinced cattleman Oscar White to let him use his property, which was ten miles away, as a launch site. The man agreed, not even asking Goddard for any money.

Goddard thrived in the isolation of his new home. Away from the distractions of Massachusetts, he made rapid improvements in his rocket design. He added a tank of pressurized nitrogen gas to the rocket in order to force the liquid oxygen and gasoline more rapidly into the large combustion chamber.

On December 30, 1930 he tested his latest rocket. It rose two thousand feet above the ground, reaching a speed of five hundred miles per hour before tilting to one side and crashing a thousand feet from the launch site.

In 1931, Goddard tested a "curtain cooling system," which sprayed burning gas and liquid oxygen against the chamber's thin metal walls. His crew added innovations of their own, building a new fuel pump, a remote-control launch system and a timer for the release of parachutes.

In 1932, Goddard left Roswell and traveled to Washington, DC. He carefully laid out his report, explaining the innovations he'd developed and the progress of his tests.

It didn't matter.

Three years before, the stock market crash had cut into the fortunes of many people, including the Guggenheims. The fund just couldn't afford any more rocket research.

Once again, Goddard had to return to Massachusetts. Once again, he became a physics professor at Clark University. But he also continued to improve his systems and patent his accomplishments. In 1934, the Guggenheim fund came through again and Goddard was able to return to Roswell.

In May 1935, Goddard tested a fifteen-foot rocket which weighed 85 pounds without fuel. It soared to 7,500 feet. Unfortunately when he tested it in the fall for Harry Guggenheim and Charles Lindbergh, the rocket failed—twice! Even more distressing to the two men was Goddard's refusal to share what he was learning with others. When scientists visited Roswell, Goddard would tell them little. The scientist published only reluctantly. Eventually Goddard agreed to allow one of his rockets to be shipped to the Smithsonian Institution. However, he made the Institution promise that no one could see it without his permission.

By now other people were beginning to take an interest in rocket research. But while Goddard was willing to accept help with various parts of his rocket, he refused to consider working with anyone else on the entire design. He spent the next few years trying to solve problems that kept coming up during his launches.

But events far beyond Goddard's control would influence his life. War clouds had begun to gather in Europe and in Asia. Germany, under Adolf Hitler, invaded Poland in September, 1939 and swiftly overran the country.

Although the United States would not enter the war until after the Japanese attack on Pearl Harbor in December 7, 1941, the military immediately began exploring possible weapons.

By then, Goddard realized that he could no longer experiment in secret. While his innovations had never been used in World War I, he believed his rockets could now be useful. He began sending letters to top leaders of the military and other government officials. Despite his efforts, the National Defense Research Committee believed Goddard would never work as part of a team, and didn't invite him to join. When Goddard finally got a meeting with members of the Army Air Corps, his trip to Washington, DC. was a waste of time. The officers barely listened to him.

Finally in 1941, Goddard was asked to help work on jet-assisted takeoff devices—Jabots—which could help planes clear the short decks of aircraft carriers. Goddard was glad to help, but disappointed that the United States military had so little interest in his rockets.

Although by the 1930s and 40s, Robert Goddard's rockets became faster and traveled further, many of his innovations would be stolen and improved upon by Nazi Germany during World War II.

Chapter 8

The Vengeance Weapon

• •

T he Germans had a much different opinion of what he'd done. While many Americans believed Robert Goddard was crazy following the publication of his original Smithsonian report in 1920, across the ocean his ideas were far more respected.

In an interview Mrs. Goddard recalled that "Many foreign nations, including Russia, Japan, Germany and Italy wrote to [Goddard] asking for his services, but he turned them all down, even though he received very little support from his own government after World War I."

Hermann Oberth was a math teacher who was born in Transylvania and moved to Germany in 1912. Despite his dark eyes, huge nose and permanently angry expression, Oberth was a calm, thoughtful man. He became so fascinated by a 1922 Heidelberg newspaper account describing Goddard's work that he wrote the scientist, "...many years I work at the problem to pass over the atmosphere of the earth by means of a rocket." Oberth asked Goddard to send him a copy of the Smithsonian booklet.

Goddard sent the book to Oberth and went back to his work developing a liquid fuel pump.

Oberth would later have the same problem as Goddard. When he wrote *By Rocket to Planetary Space*, one publisher after another rejected the book. The work went beyond just rocket theory, describing in the last section (and perhaps taking a cue from Goddard's own attention-getting ending) a huge rocket for people.

"The Model E," as Oberth called it, would carry passengers who would be strapped into their seats so they would avoid floating in the weightlessness of space.

When no one would publish it, Oberth did the job himself. In 1923, the book was a huge success, selling out several printings. It even received attention from the famous German film director Fritz Lang, whose 1929 film *The Woman in the Moon* used a rocket ship which looks something like our current space shuttle to fly from the earth to the moon.

Inspired by the increasing interest in rockets, the German automaker Opel held races with rocket-fueled cars.

But rockets also had a more sinister meaning for Germans.

Rocket societies made up of amateur astronomers, scientists, engineers and others began to develop. In 1927, the Verein fur Raumschiffahrt was formed.

Germany was in the middle of an economic collapse brought about by the country's defeat in World War I. Under the terms of the Treaty of Versailles, the country could no longer manufacture weapons. But when the treaty was signed, rockets weren't considered weapons.

In 1930, when the German government gave the Verein society $50,000 for research, the money wasn't meant for space travel. It was meant for war.

Among the society's members was Wernher von Braun. Braun was still a teenager, but he was also a brilliant engineer. He wasn't interested in weapons, he was interested in space flight. Still, he knew the best way to fund the research he dreamed of was to get money from the government. Like the other engineers in Germany who worked in the field, Braun developed a rocket with a team. He shared information with other engineers and scientists across the country and published details about his experiments.

All that work and effort bore fruit in June of 1944 when the German military began launching V-1 rockets (Vergeltungswaffe, or "Vengeance Weapons") from bases in Belgium, France and Holland. Nicknamed "buzz bombs" for the terrifying noise they made when they flew over cities, the rockets were 25 feet long. More than twenty thousand were used, with often devastating results.

For Goddard the rocket's impact was personal.

While reading a description of the V-1, Goddard realized that the German military had stolen ideas he had patented. It wouldn't be the last time.

Soon after the V-1s began descending on London, the Germans launched an even more fearsome weapon, the V-2. This was a rocket that was 47 feet high, weighed 9,000 pounds without fuel, and reached speeds of 3,600 miles per hour as it soared to a height of 60 miles. No airplane could shoot it down. No anti-aircraft shell could hit it. More than 4,000 were launched in 1945. Although they often missed their targets, entire city blocks would be flattened when their aim was true.

In March of 1945, a V-2 malfunctioned. It didn't explode. The rocket was shipped to Goddard. Inside he found some very familiar systems: turbine fuel pumps, gyroscopic stabilizers, "the curtain cooling" system. All these were items Goddard had patented, all these were devices the United States government had ignored. Much of the work had been contributed by Braun, who admitted as much when he surrendered to American forces in April of 1945.

Despite the rockets, the Germans were defeated by Allied forces, formally surrendering in May of 1945.

Still Goddard must have wondered if the war could have ended sooner, at a cost of fewer lives, if his rockets had been developed by the Allies instead of by the Germans.

World War II ended with a different type of weapon. In August of 1945, atomic bombs that had been designed and tested not far from Goddard's own test site in New Mexico dropped on the Japanese cities of Hiroshima and Nagasaki and that country's leaders formally surrendered on September 2.

But Goddard wasn't around to witness it. In June, he developed throat cancer and despite the removal of his larynx (voice box) he never recovered. Robert Goddard died on August 10.

In his honor, NASA's Goddard Space Flight Center in Greenbelt, Maryland was established on May 1, 1959. That same year, Congress voted him a Congressional Medal. In 1960, the Smithsonian Institution awarded him the Langley medal. The United States government also paid the Guggenheim Fund and Mrs. Goddard $1,000,000 for the use of his over 200 patents.

His legacy is impressive. U.S. and German scientists such as von Braun worked together after the war to combine Goddard's ideas with the V-2. Eventually the collaboration produced the mighty Saturn rockets which launched the first men to reach the moon.

And as one of those Saturn rockets carried Apollo 11 toward the moon in the summer of 1969, the *New York Times*, which had insulted him 49 years earlier in an editorial, wrote sort of a retraction.

"Further investigation and experimentation," the newspaper said, "have confirmed the findings of Isaac Newton in the 17th century, and it is now definitely established that a rocket can function in a vacuum as well as in an atmosphere. The Times regrets the error."

Tsiolkovsky, the Russian mathematician, wrote in a letter to a friend in 1911, "Man will not always stay on earth. The pursuit of light and space will lead him to penetrate the bounds of the atmosphere, timidly at first, but in the end to conquer the entire solar system."

Because of the imagination and dedication of men like Robert Goddard, those dreams are becoming real.

Established in 1959, the NASA-Goddard Space Flight Center in Greenbelt, Maryland stands as a working memorial to the man who helped make space travel possible.

Robert Goddard Chronology

- 1882, born on October 5 in Worcester, Massachusetts.
- 1899, has his first 'vision' of rocket travel.
- 1904, graduates from high school at age of 21.
- 1908, graduates from Worcester Polytechnic Institute.
- 1909, considers modified artillery rocket as best means of lifting off from earth.
- 1911, graduates from Worcester's Clark University with physics doctorate.
- 1912, hired by Princeton University as research instructor.
- 1913, contracts tuberculosis.
- 1914, applies for and receives two patents on his rocket.
- 1916, receives grant from Smithsonian Institution.
- 1918, demonstrates rockets for military.
- 1919, Smithsonian publishes Goddard's paper on rockets; it is reported in newspapers across the world.
- 1924, marries Esther Kisk.
- 1925, tests first liquid fueled rocket.
- 1926, receives second grant from Smithsonian.
- 1930, receives $25,000 a year for four years from the Guggenheim Fund on the advice of pilot Charles Lindbergh.
- 1930, moves to Roswell, New Mexico.
- 1930, conducts first static test of liquid fueled rocket.

- 1932, loses Guggenheim funding as foundation suffers financial losses in the stock market crash, returns to Massachusetts.
- 1934, regains Guggenheim funding and returns to New Mexico.
- 1935, tests two rockets which reach highest altitude ever; in a later demonstration two rockets fail.
- 1945, examination of unexploded German V-2 rocket reveals its use of many of Goddard's designs.
- 1945, dies of throat cancer.

Rocket Timeline

- **600 BC:** Ionian travelers use stars to navigate.
- **300 BC:** Antennas Diagnose writes about an imaginary trip to the moon.
- **1000:** Chinese invent rockets soon after their invention of gunpowder.
- **1600s:** Dutch mathematician Christiaan Huygens writes about a universe filled with other worlds.
- **1666:** After an apple falls on his head, Sir Isaac Newton begins formulating his laws of gravity; less than twenty years later he will write about the laws of motion.
- **1791:** After Indian troops use rockets against the British, William Congreve develops a military rocket.
- **1814:** Congreve Rockets used unsuccessfully against Fort McHenry inspire Francis Scott Key to write the lines "the rocket's red glare," in the Star Spangled Banner.
- **1860s:** Jules Verne's two popular novels *From the Earth to the Moon* and *Round the Moon* describe trips in a cyndro-projectile fired from a cannon in Florida near NASA's present-day Cape Canaveral launching site; these books will inspire many scientists including Robert Goddard.
- **1903:** Russian journal *Science Survey* publishes Konstantin Tsiolkovsky's paper explaining how a liquid fueled rocket could be used to send people outside of earth's orbit.

- **1923:** Hermann Oberth publishes *By Rocket to Planetary Space*, which builds on Goddard's work but also describes a rocket for people, which includes straps to hold them down during weightlessness.
- **1928:** German car maker Opel tests rocket fueled car which reaches record speed of 125 miles per hour at Berlin race track.
- **1929:** German filmmaker Fritz Lang's *The Woman in the Moon* shows first realistic space travel with rocket; Oberth is technical advisor.
- **1930:** Teenager Wernher von Braun begins work on what will become the V-2 rocket; by 1944 it will be capable of a speed of 3,600 miles per hour and altitude of 60 miles.
- **1961:** Soviets shoot cosmonaut Yuri Gagarin into space on April 12.
- **1969:** U.S. astronaut Neil Armstrong takes his first steps on the moon.
- **1981:** Maiden flight of NASA's Space Shuttle Columbia on April 12.
- **1986:** January 28, Challenger explodes after take-off caused by a failure of the O-rings in cold temperature.
- **1988:** America returns to space with a redesigned Discovery shuttle
- **2001:** August 10, Space Shuttle Discovery carries the third crew of U.S. Astronauts to the International Space Station.

For Further Reading

Books

Farley, Karen Clifford. *Robert H. Goddard*. Englewood Cliffs, NJ: Silver Burdett Press, 1991.

Quakenbush, Robert. *The Boy Who Dreamed of Rockets: How Robert H. Goddard Became the Father of the Space Age*. New York: Parents Magazine Press, 1978.

Streissguth, Tom. *Rocket Man: The Story of Robert Goddard*. Minneapolis, MN: Carolrhoda Books, Inc., 1995.

Web Sites

Robert Goddard - Clark University
http://www.clarku.edu/goddardfolder/goddard.html
In Depth - Dr. Goddard
http://www.gsfc.nasa.gov/indepth/about_drgoddard.html
Time 100: Scientists & Thinkers - Robert Goddard
http://www.time.com/time/time100/scientist/profile/goddard.html

Glossary of Terms

Atmosphere: boundary of air which surrounds our planet.

Combustion Chamber: a cylinder where fuels are mixed and burned to provide thrust.

Escape Velocity: the speed required for an object to move past the pull of gravity; on earth it's 25,000 miles per hour.

Gravity: the fundamental physical force responsible for the attraction of the earth, along with the moon and other large bodies.

Gunpowder: mixture of substances including charcoal and sulfur that drives bullet or fireworks forward when ignited.

Hydrogen: in liquid form, this chemical element is the lightest and most efficient possible fuel for rockets.

Oxygen: a chemical element, it is required to keep a fire burning. In space, where there isn't any oxygen, liquid oxygen is used to allow rocket fuel to burn.

Physics: the scientific study of matter, energy and how they interact.

Prototype: a test model, used as a pattern for future production.

Recoil: the act of going back under pressure, such as the recoil of a fired gun.

Thrust: force generated by rocket engine.

Index